Prologue

This tale is part of the history of a tiny village called Cambridge, located some 40 miles northeast of Albany, NY. The village was incorporated in 1866, but the "crossroads" has been inhabited since prehistoric times. Paleo Indians used a system of trails down the narrow valley, while others, coming up out of the Hudson River Valley to the west, followed a narrow defile into the valley, and camped on the banks of the Owl's Kill brook to trade and rest before continuing east thru the gaps into the nearby Green Mountains.

Cambridge was once more economically viable than it is today. The days when milk trains twice daily carried dairy and other farm products directly to markets in Boston, Albany and New York City are long past. Having long been denuded of the old growth pine grove that, with rail service, made Cambridge a "destination" for city dwellers seeking momentary respite from heat and congestion, the Village remains the size (2,000 souls) it has been these past 100 years.

While no longer a tourist destination, it is inevitably converting to bedroom community, to which down-staters repair for weekend and summer solace. Cambridge has always been a "one horse" town. Would it could stay that way. Dt

SLAVERY IN THE OLD CAMBRIDGE DISTRICT

It must have been the year 1968 when the Black Revolution in America was brought home to me. One of my former high school students was an undergraduate at a prestigious, nearby university. He determined that, whether I knew it or not, the "lecture" by Eldridge Cleaver at the said university was an event that, as an educator, I should not miss.

In those days, Cleaver was a Black Panther. Neither Cleaver nor the Panthers were of particular interest to me at the time, as neither they nor what they represented reached very deeply into Old Cambridge, a tiny community nestled in the foothills of the Green Mountains some 40 miles northeast of Albany, NY.

I attended with several others from the community. What we saw and heard presented us (or at least me) with a number of "firsts". I heard words used in public that here-to-fore I had thought, at worst, were confined to the boys locker room when the coach was absent. I learned some new nouns descriptive of white people. I learned that it was possible for a black man to travel this country with a private army. And (shades of the Nazis) I saw that said army would be allowed to screen and control the audience for a paid lecture on the campus of a major American university.

I learned that some black citizens in the United States didn't ask permission of white society, but rather made demands, which they were apparently willing to back with force and violence.

And I learned that for some black citizens "equality" was no longer the goal.

"Black Power" had arrived, along with Black Muslims, to carry the movement beyond the "dream" of the late, Rev. Martin Luther King. Where King had made a "white honky" like myself feel one part guilt and another part inspired should I entertain a happy thought toward my black brothers; Cleaver and the "Black Power" movement brought the feelings of one part puzzlement (after all, hadn't we given them… "this" and "that"?) and several parts anger because they didn't seem to appreciate what-all we had done for them.

While the rest of the Nation grappled with those turbulent days of "Black Power", the Vietnam War and the "hippy" revolution, I remained pretty much barricaded in little Cambridge. Perhaps this is why I can still write seriously of those times many years ago when this Nation and this community grappled with the moral question of Slavery; when the issue was in doubt; and of a time when we considered what to do with the "coloreds" after emancipation.

Cambridge is more of a back-water now than it was then. But while we had only a minor impact on the great, national events of those old days, I wonder if the debates and disagreements that I have found in the local records are not somewhat reflective of the thoughts and opinions running through most any small, "Yankee" Village at the time.

This essay is not a history of Slavery. It should not be considered a particularly profound or complete study of the issue as it affected Old Cambridge, no more than it should be considered the complete story of the long and compassionate relationship between the races that has evolved in this community.

It is more a "sampling" of data taken from a variety of sources, but primarily from standard sources on the question, from 18th century records of The Cambridge District, and from the files of the Washington County Post, which was for two centuries THE local weekly newspaper.

THE SHAPE OF
THE COMMUNITY

The lands which now comprise the Towns of Cambridge, Jackson and White Creek, were, in 1773, framed into The Old Cambridge District. Prior to 1773, they had simply comprised The Cambridge Patent (plus adjoining, smaller patents), as part of the very extensive County of Albany. This huge county extended to the Connecticut River on the east, through what would later become the State of Vermont.

In 1816, the towns of Cambridge, Jackson and White Creek were formed from The Old Cambridge District.

As more and more settlers moved into The Old Cambridge District, small hamlets grew up. They were the "population centers", where storehouses developed and commerce transpired. Two of the largest hamlets were North White Creek and Cambridge Corners. North White Creek centered on what is now the intersection of

Park and Main Streets in the Village of Cambridge.

North White Creek extended east toward the present intersection of Rte. 313 and W. Main, known back then as Dorr's Corners. It extended west until it reached the edge of the great swamp that once spread on both sides of the Owl Kill, the small brook that today flows through the center of Cambridge Village, and is known as Blair's Brook or Seed House Brook.

On the west side of the swamp was Cambridge Corners. This hamlet centered on the present day intersection of Main and Union Streets. It extended west toward Academy Street and Coila, known in those days as Stevenson's Corners.

Cambridge Corners straddled the major roadway of the region. The Northern Turnpike reached from Troy, NY on the south, connecting to points south and west, to Rutland, Vt. on the north, and connected to all points north and east. The Turnpike marks the boundary between the Towns of White Creek and Cambridge.

Cambridge Corners also reached south into an area of early settlement. The first Presbyterian Church was on the south edge of the current Village along the Turnpike. A few rods north was a large pond that stretched across the Valley, and which powered an early mill.

Cambridge Village poses an unusual challenge for the local historian, as well as for those officials elected to administer it, as it borders the town of Jackson on north and falls about equally into the Towns of Cambridge and White Creek.

In the late 18th and early 19th centuries, The Old Cambridge District was a dynamic region. It was for that moment in time on the "American frontier", with all of a frontier's problems and opportunities. It was uncovered by one early researcher, for example, that of the families who first settled on land in The Cambridge Patent, few stayed. And only one of the original Cambridge patentees --- the Wells clan--- actually persevered, prospered and stayed. The others apparently found greater opportunities further west as more land was opened for homesteading. This pattern of losing out to greater opportunities "further west" has plagued the Cambridge Valley to this day.

While Valley machinists pioneered in the design and manufacture of agricultural implements and knitting looms, the Valley soon lost out to Connecticut and Massachusetts due to a scarcity of water power. While the foothills of the Green Mountains provided splendidly majestic pines for the masts of Great Britain's fleet of wooden ships, the supply was limited. While the hard woods were excellent for furniture making, and for the creation of charcoal and lime (from such industry is "Black Hole Hollow" named), vast forests in the Ohio Valley soon put those industries out of business.

Fine Merino sheep were introduced in the 19th century; the hills cleared of predators, as well as habitat for predators. But after two generations, the herds were shipped with second sons to create ranches on the vast grasslands of Texas, Nebraska and Colorado. The same fate was shared by the local horse breeding industry; soon Old Cambridge was "importing" horses from the West.

The coming of the railroad in mid 19th century stimulated the dairy industry, which clings to life at this writing. The steam-powered railroad made possible the delivery of fresh products on a daily basis to large markets in Boston and New York City.

Today, even faster transportation means that produce can be maintained fresh, although shipped from all points in the Hemisphere.

Vast herds of Holsteins, maintained out of doors year round in the more gentle climates of California, Texas and New Mexico, with unlimited feed supplies growing nearby, are putting out of business the traditional, small dairy farms of The Cambridge Valley.

PROBLEMS OF RACE

This background is to suggest that residents of The Cambridge Valley have over the centuries faced many of the same social and economic problems as the rest of the United States, although perhaps not on the same scale.

Relating to the point of this essay, Old Cambridge has faced the same problems of assimilation of the races as every other part of the United States; but the scale of the problem has not been as great.

The desire for cheap help has always been here; but large scale agriculture did not develop, as it did in the South.

We have faced the same migrations of poor, white Catholic Irish as New York City and Boston, and have shown similar manifestations of prejudice and fear. The sign "Irish Need Not Apply" appeared in Cambridge businesses, the same as in Boston and New York. But in a few generations, we have fully assimilated those immigrants who chose to stay in the Valley, although most seem to have moved on west for the greater opportunities.

The same is true with the Italian immigrants. A few families survive from those that came to the Valley in the 19th century to build the railroad and the Village water system. They are fully assimilated.

More to the point of this essay, black or African-American residents have been in the Valley from the beginning of the European settlement of these former Indian lands. They have progressed from being our chattel possessions to being our friends, neighbors and Christian brothers and sisters.

The famous Wells clan, the only family named on The Cambridge Patent who settled here, were slave owners. Those early settlers of Dutch descent who farmed in the Hoosick Valley and south in the Cambridge Valley utilized black slaves in their agricultural endeavors. There is evidence that at least some of the ministers who served the Cambridge Valley also owned blacks as slaves. It is even likely that the first Dutch farmers in the south valley enslaved or attempted to enslave the Mohican and Abinaki Indians whose lands they acquired.

Slavery in the early days of Cambridge was not as widespread as in other, larger "Yankee" communities. But slavery was here, was extensive, and was practiced by the "best" and wealthiest families.

LOCAL SLAVE SALE

In May, 1873, Thomas B. Ashton, a descendent of the early Methodist family that settled in Ash Grove, Town of White Creek, made public a document recording an ancient slave sale in the Old Cambridge District. It had been conducted for his ancestor, James Ashton.

Thomas Ashton allowed the record of the transaction to be published in The Washington Count Post, as a matter of public curiosity. The documents read:

"Received from James Ashton in cash and vallew (sic.) to the amount of 55 lb. one shilling and six pence, being in part for "Shu", the wench and child sold him.

"I say RCVD this 14th day of April, 1789. (signed) William Perine."

The following year, 1790, Perine signed another such receipt, as James Ashton apparently paid for female slave and brood in installments.

James Ashton was a hero of the American Revolution and one of the founders of the second Methodist Church in the United States, established in Ash Grove. But like George Washington, Thomas Jefferson and many other early American heroes, he owned other human beings as slaves.

Like James Ashton, most revered founders of this community kept slaves. But Old Cambridge did not originate the practice, nor did the community continue the it nearly as long as did white settlers in other parts of the world.

Anyone who has ever sat through a production of Arthur Miller's chilling drama "The Crucible" knows that, while not necessarily widely practiced, slave holding was common-place among the affluent in the Massachussetts Bay Colony, including the ministers in that Theocracy.

The first European to practice enslavement on this continent may have been Christopher Columbus, himself. Richard E. Irby Jr., in his "Chronology of Slavery", notes that Columbus shipped 500 Indians to Spain to be sold as slaves.

Just about every segment of the European continent that sent explorers to The New World sent back enslaved Indians--- those they didn't massacre in order to secure their lands!

As early as the 1500s, the Spanish were importing black slaves to serve their sugar cane plantations in the Caribbean region.

SOME SLAVE
HISTORY

The history of man's enslavement of man is long and depressingly cruel. But man's resistance to this infamous practice is also long, and inspiring.

In 1563, the Queen of England condemned taking any African "without his free consent"; but on the other hand, she took shares in the slaving practiced by English entrepreneurs of that day.

By the end of the 16th century, Irby estimates that there were 900,000 African slaves in the Americas, mostly engaged in Spanish colonies in the Indies that produced sugar from cane.

In the 17th century beginnings of the tobacco industry in Virginia, Irby finds that growers took any sort of help they could get. He found a record of the sale of 140 white female convicts from Britain who were sold in Jamestown, Virginia in 1619 "against their weight in tobacco". They had no rights at all during the course of their sentences for "crimes" in the mother country.

Even the legendary "Squanto", who in 1621 taught the Pilgrims how to farm and thereby saved them from starvation, did so after escaping from slavery.

According to Irby, in 1637 the Massachusetts militia massacred a Pequod village at Mystia, killing about 600, drowning

the surviving males and selling the women and
children as slaves.

These Pequod Indian slaves were
transported to the Indies on the first American
slave ship, the "Desire".

In 1641, Massachusetts made the first
attempt to outlaw slavery, although one who
committed certain crimes could still be
enslaved.

Meanwhile, legal slavery was growing in
the tobacco industry of Virginia. By the late
17th century, the slave trade in Britain was
wide open, with an estimated 300,000 African
slaves exported over the last 20 years of the
century.

Irby relates that from 1700 to 1786 some
610,000 African slaves were transported to
Jamaica, with a death rate estimated at 30
percent.

By 1715, African slaves made up 24
percent of the population of Virginia. By 1724,
according to Irby, African slaves out-numbered
whites in (south) Carolina two to one.

RESISTANCE
IN THE NORTH

By 1741, New York City, which had begun
as a Dutch city, had experienced two slave
revolts, both of which were put down with
bloody force, including hangings and burnings
at the stake.

New England developed early as a region
of sea-faring merchants. This skill they
readily adapted to the slave trade. By 1750,
Massachusetts had 63 distilleries producing gin
and rum, which was shipped to Africa in trade
for slaves to sell south.

Resistance to the poison of slave trading
was slowly growing, however. Even though some
Quakers owned slaves, those who dealt in the
slave trade in 1761, were excluded from the
Society of Friends.

In March 1775, the fight was joined by
Thomas Paine, the famous rebel of the American
war for Independence. In an essay appearing in
the March 8 issue of the Pennsylvania Journal

and Weekly Advertiser, Paine wrote that "African nations inhabit fertile countries, are industrous farmers, enjoy plenty, and lived quietly… before the Europeans debauched them with liquors, and bribing them against one another….

"By such wicked and inhuman ways the English are said to enslave towards one hundred thousand yearly; of which thirty thousand are supposed to die by barbarous treatment in the first year…. So much innocent blood have the managers and supports of this inhuman trade to answer for to the common Lord of all!"

GRADUALCHANGE

The Quakers regarded slavery as an evil. The American Revolution brought a general consciousness raising about the rights of men (if not the rights of women).

Many persons were offended by their neighbors who held human slavery as one of the privileges of wealth. Many insisted that slaves should be taught to read and write, claiming that next to life and liberty, education was the greatest blessing bestowed upon mankind. Gradually colored children were allowed to attend the public schools.

In 1830, John B. Ruswoom was graduated from Boudoin College, Maine, the first colored to graduate from college in America.

The NY State Convention of 1821 denied the free Negro without property the right of suffrage, and the old property qualification was retained as it affected this small body of voters until outlawed by the 15th amendment of the Federal Constitution in 1870.

About 1840 the free Negro with property in NY State was allowed to vote in some NY election districts. Women of any race were not.

The Quakers of Old Cambridge and White Creek made slavery very unpopular here. Most had been freed before the law gave them their unconditional freedom. But in most cases, they were loyal to their old masters and remained in their service as paid servants In 1785, about two years after the close of the Revolution, NY State passed a law prohibiting the sale of slaves. In 1788 this law was amended to prevent the import of slaves for sale. These laws, however, did not prevent the holding of persons as slaves.

In 1790 there were approx. 22,000 slave children in NY State. In 1799 a law was passed to free all female slaves after July 4, 1799, who had reached the age of 25 years and all males over the age of 28, unless incapable of earning their subsistence.

By 1808, the slave population of NY State had dropped to about 15,000.

WHAT TO DO
WITH FREEDMEN

Thomas Paine wanted to end the practice, but he had no better idea of how to reverse the process than many leaders of the century that followed.

"The great question may be, 'what should be done with those who are enslaved already?" He acknowledged that turning free the old and infirm would also be cruel and unjust. He suggested that those who had enjoyed their labors during "their better days" should keep and humanely treat them through their final days, which is what came to be practiced with the slaves of Old Cambridge.

He thought perhaps the freed slaves might be sent to the American frontiers where they "might sometime form useful barrier settlements….

"Thus they may become interested in the public welfare," he reasoned, "And assist in promoting it; instead of being dangerous, as now they are, should any enemy promise them a better condition."
The idea of "exporting" freed slaves tantalized and perplexed humanitarians up to and through

the Civil War. It continues to this day, with the occasional Black Nationalist calling for a "homeland" within continental US.

Prophetically, Paine suggested that "…past treatment of Africans must naturally fill them with abhorrence of Christians; lead them to think our religion would make them more inhuman savages, if they embraced it…:

"Are we not, therefore, bound in duty to him and to them to repair these injuries, as far as possible, by taking some proper measure to instruct, not only the slaves here, but the Africans in their own countries?"

NEW YORK CHANGES

Only four of the northern states abolished slavery in the 18th century, although this does not mean that thereafter there were no black slaves in those states. Vermont apparently passed such legislation in 1777, although Vermont was not even a state at the time--- only in rebellion against the rightful owner of the land, New York.

Massachusetts and Pennsylvania followed suit in 1780, and Connecticut in 1803.

Pennsylvania received a big push from the Quaker population. The first anti-slavery society in America was formed in Philadelphia in April of 1775. Not surprisingly, Thomas Paine was a member.

New York was not at the forefront of the anti-slavery movement. Although restrictions were placed upon the practice in the late 18th century that led to the freeing of many local slaves, the practice was not abolished until 1827. Of course, after that time there remained the long and fierce battle to protect escaped slaves that fled north; and to prevent northern slaves from being sold south.

According to George DeWan, writing in a history of Long Island, New York was the largest slave holding state in the North. And like the other states, NY ended slavery gradually, taking some three decades to get the job done.

When asked if the policy of gradually freeing the slaves had been a success, one scholar replied cryptically, "It certainly beats the Civil War…."

As in Pennsylvania, DeWan found that the Quakers led the antislavery effort in New York. Even after the Revolutionary War and the Declaration of Independence, which contains the phrase "…all men are created equal", the slave holders up the Hudson Valley were reluctant to part with this important source of labor.

The New York Manumission Society, of which many were Quakers, was organized in 1785.

DeWan noted that one of the biggest problems for authorities was that the slave owners of New York often chose to sell their slaves in the South, rather than lose their investment through manumission, even though such sales were illegal.

One researcher noted a sharp drop in New York's black population after 1800, due largely to the illegal practice of selling blacks south.

In Albany, abolitionists of New York won their first big victory in 1799, when the State Legislature passed an act for the gradual abolition of slavery. The law provided that children born in New York to slave mothers after July 4 of that year would serve their mother's owner only until the age of 28 (males) and 25 (females).

At the beginning of the 19th century, manumission became common, particularly in wills. Runaways also became common, as young males, primarily, were unwilling to remain indentured until the age of 28.

Soon those engaged in labor-intensive business found that their work forces might contain black slaves working side by side with freedmen and those young slaves serving out indenturements, as well as indentured whites.

In 1817, the Legislature passed the act to end slavery in 10 years (1827).

IMPACT ON
OLD CAMBRIDGE

The impact of these laws was certainly felt in the Cambridge Valley, as illustrated by the dates on the numerous manumission papers which were recorded.

Probably the most famous home of Old Cambridge is that
built by Edmund Wells in 1787. The Great Northern Turnpike was
built in front of it. Over the front door was a large sun dial.

Folklore has it that fleeing slaves were taught to look for it, as
a haven on their trek to freedom in Canada.

Later, the Wells home possibly was a stop along the underground railway.
Edmund was the only signer of the Cambridge Patent to settle here. Edmund and his sons fought for the Revolution at the Battles of White Plains and Walloomsac, (Bennington to the uninitiated).The great door below the sun dial probably did open to fugitive slaves, just as it had to harried patriots.

But at the time of the Revolution, the Wells family, too, owned
slaves. From 1801 through 1807, Austin Wells recorded that one of his slaves gave birth almost every year.

The handsome red brick Home of Edmund Wells can be seen today half a mile below Cambridge Village along the former Great Northern Turnpike. There is a circular decoration over the door, a hex symbol or a circular sundial. The house was built in 1787. Edmund, Yale graduate, fought in the battle of Walloomsac in the American Revolution. Edmund died in 1805. This information is according to a letter written in 1940 by descendent Austin Wells and published in the Washington County Post.

Edmund Wells' home was right on the Turnpike, the major highway into Canada from NY State. Austin Wells believed that the home was used by soldiers at the time of the Battle of Walloomsac. It was said to be a haven for American soldiers.

Certainly it would have been, as so many Wells fought for the Rebel cause. However, its position on the British line of march to and from the Battle of Walloomsac suggests that it was also at least visited by British soldiers.

At the time of the Civil War and the Underground Railroad, the house was also on a major route for slaves being shepherded into Canada. Local legend has it that the traffickers came to recognize the sun dial over the door as a sign of safe haven for their black charges.

Frank McClellan, who was an avid local historian, used his early family connections to gain access to Town of White Creek records that have since been lost. He borrowed the records from Henry Perry in December, 1940.

According to Frank McClellan, one of the largest land owners in the Old Cambridge District was Philip Van Ness. His manor house stood near the John L. Pratt home (1940) at Buskirk's Bridge. According to the local census of 1790, six slaves lived on the Van Ness Manor. John Faulkner (location of house unknown) owned five slaves. Louis H. Veile, four; Peter Veile, two; and John Brott owned three.

The Viele family lived on the south side of the Hoosick River between Buskirk's Bridge and Eagle Bridge. This home was later owned by the Gooding family.

LOCAL SLAVE

BURIAL GROUNDS

According to McClellan, there was a traditional story about an old slave cemetery on the Van Ness/Pratt place. It was said to be located near a south fence along an orchard. Sometime after Island Hill Cemetery was established near Buskirk's Bridge, the remains were removed and placed along the middle driveway of Island Hill. The Van Ness monument is also located along this drive, so perhaps the Van Ness slave graves are located in the family reservation. There are no markers.

The Knickerbocker family of Schaghticoke and other families are alleged to have buried their slaves in their private burial lots, and erected markers. However, it seems to have been more the custom to bury slaves in unmarked graves in the paths through and around family burial lots.

Another source has shown this writer what legend says is the Ashton slave burial ground in Ash Grove, White Creek. It is said to have been located after the turn off Ash Grove Road to Pumpkin Hook, on the left as the road ascends the first grade.

McClellan recalled seeing stocks in the basement of the Knickerbocker Mansion, presumably for slaves and any troublesome people.

In the pre-revolutionary days, McClellan believed that there was no such abuse of slaves has was reported on the South, there being fewer and it being more of a personal relationship. During colonial British rule it was common for men of property to own slaves.   One of largest landowners in the District was Philip Van Ness. His
manor house was near Buskirk's. The 1790 census lists him with six slaves.

Johannes Van Buskirk, with others, in 1724 built a bridge
and founded the hamlet of Buskirk's Bridge. Cornelius Buskirk, in 1794 at Schaghticoke, acknowledged an illegitimate child born to his slave.

And so the old records go, year by year, matter of factly recording
the births of the children of captivity in Old Cambridge.
As a matter of curiosity, I pursued the slave mother Nan through
the record, and not once did I find where she gave birth to a male
child.

These examples were taken from an Old Cambridge minute book from
1773.

Other similar entries prove beyond doubt that slavery was an

accepted practice among the early wealthy land
owners of this area.
The 1790 census reveals that there were 22
slave owners in Old Cambridge
Dist.

Some other examples:

The Whiteside family were the pioneers of
West Cambridge. William Whiteside certified
that on the 10th day of Feb., 1802 a male child
named Ben was born of a female slave owned by
him.

The Wendells lived in the big yellow
house on Main St. where Academy joins it.
Morrison and son George McGeoch were recent
owners.

Cornelius Wendell was a prominent local
lawyer and judge. He served in the State
Legislature. He also had a slave named Phillis
that bore a Negro boy named Jack.

The Lake family, of early Dutch
extraction, has been prominent in White Creek
since before there was a White Creek. Gerrit
Lake certified that on Jan. 15 1799, his female
slave named Deyan was delivered of a female
child ... and on the 17th of Sept. 1802, the
same slave was delivered of a male child named
Harry.

John Younglove is buried in the front row
of the old cemetery on
Park St. Younglove was the leader of the local
rebels of the Revolutionary
War days.

After the Revolution, "Judge" Younglove
decided who had been loyal
to the cause and could return to his farm
without paying taxes
for the war years and who had not been
sufficiently loyal and whose
land should, therefore, be forfeited and given
to one who had been
a better servant of the Revolution.

And yet, Younglove's passion for liberty
did not extend to his
own household. The old minute book for the
period reads, "On the 28th day of
February 1801, was born a female child, of a
slave named Nan the

property of John Younglove Esq."

EVEN PASTORS

Rev. John Dunlap was an early minister at the United Presbyterian Church. That is where the Baptists were in 2002. In 1813, Dunlap manumitted his slave named Nell. Richard Feus, who lives in the former Dunlap house on South Union St., has found records indicating that Nell continued on as the Dunlap house servant until she died.

David Simpson, of the town of White Creek manumitted his Negro man slave named Henry Van Schaick on Oct. 8, 1816.

SLAVE BIRTHS

Few records from the early days of the Old Cambridge District have survived. Neglect, improper disposal and vandalism are common culprits. The fact is it was the 1920s before the first archive storage room was built in the Town of Cambridge. And it was the 1980s before a serious effort began to collect and protect the paper history of the towns.

In those early days there were no public buildings. Meetings were held in ale houses and private homes. Over the generations, these public documents came to be considered by descendents as the private property of the families, although a good case can be made for the return of every public record to the public trust.

What began as an effort by conscientious, pioneer public servants to protect public documents and records has become, in too many cases, a major way for those documents to be lost. Often descendents do not recognize the old papers for what they are; too often, when the old homes are sold, the ancient public documents have followed the paper trail into the closest landfill, to be lost forever.

In still other cases, those same dedicated public servants, recognizing that the local towns were in no position to protect important documents, have entrusted them to the State Archive and Records Center, New York State Library, Albany.

For anyone seeking more information on local slavery than is contained in this document, that is a very good place to look.

And yet, there is one ancient document from the formative time of The Old Cambridge District that provides at least a glance into this infamous practice: the minute book for the year 1773.

Jeremiah Stillwell is thought to have been a local patent medicine man. However he made his money, he was sufficiently affluent to afford slaves. Born on July 5 1805, his female slave (name not given) bore him a male child (name not given).

John Younglove, one of the major local heroes of the Revolutionary War, owned a slave named Nan. On February 25 1801, Nan, "the property of John Younglove, esq., bore him a female child that he named "Dean".

Cornelius Wendell, whose son would grow up to be known as "the President's printer", was a prominent resident on the west end of Cambridge Corners. "On the third day of July last" his slave Phillis gave birth to a "negroe" (sic) boy named Jack by his mother".

William Whiteside, founder of one of the most prominent families in the history of West Cambridge and Easton and a major financial contributor to the local effort in the American Revolution, was also the owner of slaves. In the 1773 minute book of the Town, Whiteside "certifies that on the 10th day of Feb. 1802, a male child named Ben was born of a female slave owned by him".

Austin Wells, of the only family named on the original Cambridge Charter to settle here, was also an owner of slaves. He certified that "…on the 28th of October 1801, was born in his house of a Negro slave of his named Nan, a female child named Dolly".

We know that Wells had more than one slave, and that he kept slaves for a number of years, because the old minute book holds a record of the birth of a female child to "Nan" on March 1, 1807. Nan was owned by Austin Wells and the child, which would also belong to Wells, was named Sibbel. Wm. McAuley certified that on the sixth day of October, 1802 was born a male child named Dink of his slave named Mary.

In the record for 1803, Austin Wells again certifies that on the 18th day of Sept "…was born in his house of his Negro slave named Nan (another) female Negro child", this one named Judy.

"Born in my house 30 March 1809 to my Negro slave Nan, a female Negro child named Dina," so certified Austin Wells.

Again, on 17 May 1810, Austin Wells' slave Nan gave birth, this time to a child named Nell, evidently yet another female.

Female slaves faced a kind of "double slavery": One for the color of their skin and the other because in those times even white females had very few of the rights accorded free men.

One of the oldest and most prominent families in early Cambridge history is the Greens. At least one, Thomas, owned slaves. The record indicates that on June 25, 1804 his slave "Jenn bore a male child named Pomp".

George Barber certified that on the 5 September 1803, was born to his female slave called "Dine" a male child named Andrew.

On Sept. 20, 1808, Thomas Green's slave Jean bore a male child named Prince.

Peter Perine had more than one slave and, based upon his transaction with James Ashton, perhaps bought and sold slaves as a business. On October 25, 1801, his female slave Rachel bore a male son named Charles. On December 30, 1804, his female slave Leney bore him a male child named Edenborough. Isaac Perine, on 30 Sept. 1804, recorded that his female slave Bine was delivered of a female child named Margaret.

Joseph Gilberts reported that on 18 April 1805, his female child Almirer born to his female slave Nan.

The Cornell name is another old and prominent local family name that thrives to this day. Indeed, the local Cornells are a branch of the family that founded Cornell University. But in 1804, at least one member of the family was a slave owner. Paul Cornell certified that on the 8th of November, "…was born of his female slave Ann a female child named Fancy".

And on the 17th of September, 1802 "…the same slave was delivered of a male child named Harry, and also on the 5 day April 1805 the same slave was delivered of a female child named Melinda".

By those who regarded slaves in those days much as a dairyman regards his Holsteins in these days, it is not hard to see how the practice could be made lucrative.

"This may certify that born in the house and the property of James Fort a black male child named Han. Abraham T. Fort, guardian to James Fort."

Abraham Van Tuyl certified that on September 22, 1806, his female slave Rachel delivered a child, Susan.

Van Tuyl was a farmer in the lower valley and a major slave-owner in the area. Abraham Van Tuyl certified that on 14 January, 1807 his female slave Rachel delivered yet another female child, Dean.

MANUMISSION

OF SLAVES

In the early 1800s, local families steadily divested themselves of their slaves. But it was not an easy process. The slaves were to be able to provide their own subsistence, lest one man's freed slave became a drain on the public welfare.

John Younglove was one of those who so sought to divest himself. The following record is also from an early Town of Cambridge minute book:

"Whereas it is represented to us the subscribers being a majority of the overseers of the poor and two of the justice of the peace of the town of Cambridge, said county of Washington, by John Younglove Esq., that he desires to manumit his Negro slave, named Prince Acker. We therefore certify that he appears to be about the age of thirty-one and consequently under fifty years of age and in our opinion of sufficient ability to maintain himself.

"Given under our hands in said Cambridge this 26th day of March, 1802.

(signed) Reuben Pride and Jesse e Fairchild (overseers)

Edmund Wells and James Towne (justices)"

On the other hand, there were those in local government who had the responsibility to see that abandoned or freed former slaves did not starve. Theirs was a double responsibility, for they seem to have felt just as strongly that tax dollars were not to be squandered. Theophilus Carter was paid two (real) dollars per month for providing care and training for an abandoned slave that did not meet the criteria (able to support self) for manumission.

"These are to certify that Theophilus Carter late of this town, merchant, has received from the overseers of the poor at the rate of two dollars for month for keeping and maintaining a female Negro child up to the last Tuesday of March last, said child having been abandoned and entered on the Town Clerk's book agreeable to law for a certificate of said abandonment filed in the comptrollers office of this state. Given under my hand in the town of Troy this 6 Feb. 1804. David Henry, Overseer of Poor

"I Theophilus Carter do hereby certify that on the 26 day of Dec. 1803, my female slave Phebe was delivered of a male child, since called Pat and I hereby further give notice that I have abandoned and do hereby abandon my right to the service of such a male child as aforesaid.

On 1804, Jesse Fairchild gave notification that he was abandoning an infant son born to one of his slaves.

"I Jesse Fairchild of the Town of Cambridge in the County of Washington State of New York… do certify that Jack a Negro boy to whose service I am entitled, was born in my house on 25 January last, that his mother Chriss is a slave and now my property and I do hereby abandon the said Negro boy Jack to the overseers of the poor of the town of Cambridge aforesaid as a pauper of the said town and all right which I have to the services of the said Negro boy.

31 march 1804"

William McAuley reported that on 10/6/1802 his female slave Mary bore a male child named Dick. "...And I do hereby further give notice that I have abandoned and do hereby abandon my right to the service of such male child a...."

Philip Smith of Cambridge manumitted his "Negro man", Sam in 1806. The Overseers of the poor certified that Sam was under the age of 50 yrs. and able to provide for himself.

Manumission to fulfill the desires of deceased owners became commonplace. Here is an example.

"We the subscribers being three of the executors of the last will and testament of Philip Smith, deceased, do hereby certify that in pursuance of an act of the legislature of the state of New York entitled "an act concerning slaves and servants" passed the 8th day of April 1801 and in pursuance of a verbal agreement made between the said Philip Smith deceased in his life time and Lunn his Negro man slave, we the said executors do manumit the said Negro man slave called Lunn. ...Wendell, Asahel Morris, Catalina Smith"

In 1801, Jeremiah Stillwell took advantage of the new law to manumit two slaves.

"I Jeremiah Stillwell ... do hereby manumit my Negro man slave named Salem Bandeau and my Negro woman slave named Arabella, his wife in pursuance of an act of the legislature of the State of New York..., the eighth day of April 1801. Jeremiah Stilwell, in the presence of David Simpson."

William McAuley manumitted Samuel on 8 April 1801. But he held slaves until at least 1814, because that is the year he recorded his slave Peg giving birth to the male child Harry 10 November 1814.

Austin Wells waited until 1813 to record his first manumission, on February 13th, the female "Negro" named "Nan" or "Hannah" who had bore him so many female slave children.

John Gordon manumitted his slave Harry on 11 march 1813.

Peter Perine did the same for his "woman slave" named Rachel on 3 march 1813, as certified by Jonathan Dorr, Judge. (11 April 1814).

And manumitting a slave in 1913 was the Presbyterian minister: "I, John Dunlap, do hereby manumit my female slave named Nell 9 April 1813".

Three years later, David Simpson, of another prominent local family, did the same. He manumitted his "Negro man slave named Henry Van Schaick" on October 8, 1816.

The following is the complete account of the Ashton slave purchase, as it appeared in The Washington County Post in 1873. Thomas D. Ashton brought in the document, as a matter of curiosity:

"Received from James Ashton in cash and vallew (sic) to the amount of 55 lb. one shilling and six pence, being in part for Shu the wench and child sould (sic) him I say. RCVD this 14th day of April, 1789. (signed) William Perine.

RCVD from James Ashton in cash and vallew (sic) to the amount of nineteen lb. 18 shillings and 6 d (?), being in full for Shu the wench and child sold him. I say RCVD by me this 30th of March, 1790. (Signed) William Perine

Thomas B. Ashton's comment: "I feel thankful that should the iniquity of the fathers be visited upon the children it extends only to the third and fourth generation."

LOCAL
MANUMISSION

In the Old Cambridge District, before a slave could be manumitted, two overseers of the poor and two justices of the peace had to certify that the slave would not become a burden to society.

William McAuley in 1802 owned a female slave named Mary, who bore him a male child slave named Dick, which he sought to abandon.

Abandonment, like manumitting, was strictly controlled for the general good of the society. There was no welfare state in 1802. Each District had poor-masters, whose job it was to see that the deserving poor were cared for.

But this came directly from local taxes. It cost the tax-payers two real dollars)per month, for example, to hire the keep of an abandoned slave child. Therefore, the poor-masters would not allow an owner to make a former slave the responsibility of his neighbors. Owners were to be held accountable for those slave unable to fend for themselves, if manumitted.

The merchant Theophilus Carter, for example, received from the overseers of the poor two dollars a month for keeping and maintaining a female Negro child that had been abandoned.

Each man had an obligation to maintain his slaves. The committee determined whether a slave could be manumitted, based upon whether that slave could provide a living for himself.

One of the most interesting of the slaves of the community--- just because we know something about his life--- is Salem Bedeau (or Bedo). Salem was born at Seabrook, Connecticut

about the year 1779. He was owned by Jeremiah
Stillwell of Cambridge. Salem is described as
being about 5 ft. 8 inches tall. He was
apparently manumitted by Stillwell 24 Aug 1810,
although the record indicates that Stillwell
tried to do it earlier (I Jeremiah Stillwell ...
do hereby manumit my man slave named Salem
Bedeau and my Negro woman slave named Arabella,
his wife in pursuance of an act of the
legislature of New York the eighth day of April,
1801. Jeremiah Stilwell, in the presence of
David Simpson).

Thereafter, Salem served as sextant (or
graveyard keeper) of the First Presbyterian
Churchyard at Park and Main. Salem is buried in
the extreme southeast corner of that burying
ground, beneath a simple, recently repaired
stone.

INDENTUREMENT OF COLORED CHILD

TOWN OF WHITE CREEK, 1817

"*This indenture made this fifth day
of May one thousand eight hundred and
seventeen witnesseth that George Barker
and David Simpson overseers of the poor
of the Town of White Creek in the County
of Washington and State of New York by &
with the consent of Austin Wells and
William Briggs two of the Justices of
the Peace of said County whose names are
hereunto subscribed have put & placed
and by these presents do put and place
Cordelia Benani a poor child of couler
of the aforesaid township apprentice to
Thias Johnson Jr. the Town of Cambridge
county and state aforesaid, Tanner (???)
aged three years three months and
sixteen days with him to dwell and to
serve from the day of the date hereof
until the said apprentice shall
accomplish her full age of eighteen
years according to the Laws in that case
made and provided during all which term
the said apprentice her said master
faithfully shall serve in all lawful
business according to her power (wit???)
& abilities honestly orderly and
obediently in all things demean and
behave herself towards her said master
and all his .... during the said
term.....*

"And the said Thias Johnson Jr. doth for himself his heirs executors administrators and assigns covenant and agree to and with the said overseers of the poor and every of them and their and every of their successors in office for the time being by these presents the said Cordelia Binani the said apprentice in the art and mystery of housewifery--- will teach and instruct or cause to be taught and instructed in the best way and manner that he can and shall and will teach or cause to be taught the said apprentice to read and write a suitable hand for an apprentice of her condition in life and during all the term aforesaid find provide and allow unto the said apprentice competent and sufficient meat drink and apparel lodging washing and all other things necessary and fit for an apprentice and also shall and will provide for the said apprentice that she be not any way a charge to the said town but of & from all charge shall & will save the said town harmless during the said term and at the end thereof shall and will provide allow and deliver unto the said apprentice double---- apparel one suit of which is to be new and fit to wear on holy days and one new bible.
In witness whereof the parties aforesaid to these presents indentures have interchangeably put their hands and seals the day and year just written---
Signed sealed and delivered
In the presence of ---
Wm. Briggs
Thias Johnson

George Barker
David Simpson
Overseers of the poor

"We William Briggs and Austin Wells
two of the Justices of the Peace for the
County of Washington residing in the
Town of White Creek do hereby declare
our assent to the binding Cordelia
Benoni apprentice to Thias Johnson Jr.
according to the form and effect of the
above written Indenture given under our
hands the 5th day of May 1817."

"Whereas it is represented to us
the subscribers being a majority of the
overseers of the poor and two of the
justice of the peace of the town of
Cambridge, said county of Washington, by
John Younglove Esq., that he desires to
manumit his Negro slave, named Prince
Acker. We therefore certify that he
appears to be about the age of thirty-
one and consequently under fifty years
of age and in our opinion of sufficient
ability to maintain himself.
Given under our hands in said Cambridge
this 26th day of March, 1802.
(signed) Reuben Pride and Jesse e
Fairchild (overseers)
        Edmund Wells and James Towne
(justices)"

Slavery & The Civil War
Why Southern
Yeomen Fought
In "The Land They Fought For" by Clifford
Dowdey (Doubleday, 1955) he found that at the

time of the Civil War, less than 1 % of
Southerners were wealthy plantation owners.
Less than 10% of the population owned slaves.
So, why would these yeomen Southerners with no
real stake in it fight to retain slavery? The
answer, of course, is "they didn't"!

Dowdey concluded that they were drawn into
the war "…by the parochial nature of their
society, the love of homeland and respect for
the ruling class, as well as by "…the all-
inclusive nature of the attacks upon their
society from without."

At the time, the South was in transition,
from an agrarian to an industrial economy.
Slaves were becoming less necessary. Much
manumission took place in the South before the
war. Statesman John Randolph of Virginia, for
example, manumitted some 400 slaves---worth half
a million dollars---before the war, and had the
money to send them back to Africa.

In fact, before the Civil War broke out,
so many Virginians had freed their slaves that,
in some counties, there were more freedmen than
FREE men.

WHY OLD CAMBRIDGE
FOUGHT THE CIVIL WAR
When in the spring of 1861, President
Abraham Lincoln called
for 75,000 volunteers to put down the rebellion
in the South, Old Cambridge responded.

The Old Washington County Post, then
publishing from the second floor of the Crocker
Building on Main St. by the new railroad,
reported that New York State was to furnish
30,000 men. The Legislature had appropriated $3
Million to finance them.

"The war has begun. A crisis is upon us,"
thundered the war editor R. King Crocker.
''There is nor can be but one response," wrote
the former school teacher. "He who refuses to
respond to the call of his government in this
hour of extreme peril is no more nor less than
a coward or traitor."

Strong words for a populace that was in a
general way indifferent to the conflict.

True, when the Massachusetts industrialists financed the removal of armed radicals to the territory of Kansas, to guarantee that it would become a state free of Slavery, some locals were drawn in; however very few felt touched by that aspect of the controversy.

But to save the Union? In that same issue of the Old WCP, Editor Crocker also included an account of the surrender of Fort Sumter on April 14. The shots fired at a relief squad trying to reach Fort Sumter on the South Carolina coast was the catalyst. The shots roused the community.

The issue of southern slavery would challenge local Civil War boosters and recruiters from beginning to end. That New York had settled its own slave issue decades before might account for that ambivalence.

Surely, amongst those who entered the war at Lincoln's first call were some who were willing to offer their own lives in order to end slavery in the United States. Most, however, seemed to have enlisted out of a sense of patriotism, to defend the Union.

And it was this call to the defense of the Union that was used to rouse local recruits throughout the long and incredibly bloody conflict. Never was slavery the burning issue.

On June 6, the 22nd Regiment was mustered into Federal service. There were 10 companies in all, totaling roughly 1,000 men. Three came from Essex County, two from Warren, one from the Town of Hoosick and four from Washington County.

Co, B was raised in Fort Edward, Co. G in Whitehall, Co. H in Sandy Hill (Hudson Falls) and Co. D in Old Cambridge.

Walter Phelps of Warren County was the first colonel and regimental commander. Gordon F. Thomas of Essex was lieutenant colonel.

John J. McKie Jr. of Cambridge was major of the regiment.

JR Fisher reported from Williams College that the Rev. Mr. Morley advised the drilling students of a "secesh" in the south of town. The 100 man company of students repaired there and told him to recant or face tar and feathers.

Fisher said that he recanted. Two in Adams were also so cured.

For the first time slavery is raised in the local community as a war issue. As a "divine institution," it is attacked from the pulpit.

At the end of June a former colored resident, Cornelius Jackson, returned to the Valley, having narrowly escaped enslavement while in the South.

In December the question of the emancipation of the slaves dominated page one of the WCP. Normally this page was full of ads and serialized novels of romance, morality and sentiment. But with the beginning of the war, page one presented the war on the national level.

Crocker thought that Robert Vallandigham, the leader of the Copperhead movement in the north, should be in jail with Slidell and Mason.

That February, General Ulysses S. Grant, fighting on the Western Front, captured the Forts Donnellson on the Cumberland River and Henry on the Tennessee. Forty of the rebel officers captured were imprisoned in Albany, NY. Union soldiers took pleasure in taunting them, asking them if they still believed that 1 reb could whip 5 yanks.

Editor R.K. Crocker's Union ticket held together in the White Creek caucus that March. He described the fight as "A struggle between those whose love of the Union enables them to forego party for their country... and those... that can see nothing but 'nigger, nigger' in anything but that which goes under the stolen title of 'Democratic ticket."

Lincoln at this point offered a gradual, state by state abolition of slavery. Editor Crocker admitted that slavery was the key issue, and that it would "exercise a controlling influence on the final settlement."

April 1862, President Lincoln signed a bill abolishing slavery in the District of Columbia. And that April one of the community's better known establishments, the Cambridge Valley House, from which so many soldiers were recruited, went bankrupt. J.J. Gray bought it under a foreclosure proceeding, probably to recover a mortgage on it. This in modern times was known as "The Brick Hotel" at the corner of Main and Park Sts.

LOCALS IN
EARLY CAMPAIGNS

At the end of April a letter arrived from S.M. Peters describing the role of the 93rd Regiment in the Peninsular campaign.

"We landed at Fortress Monroe on the first of April with the expectation of advancing by rapid marches to the City of Richmond. Two weeks have passed and we are still in sight of the Fortress. The delay is very vexatious to me, but the delay is unavoidable.

"Why, I am not permitted to say."

"The lords of the soil have fled, and the poor slaves remain in possession of the few shanties their vandal masters have left standing.... When our splendid columns sweep past their shanties, the music of the bands call forth all their admiration.

S.M. Peters, Drums Major for the 93rd NYIVI, would later die in combat in the battle for Petersburg and Richmond, Va.

Capt. Milliman of the 22nd NY, Company D, reported numerous "contrabands" were coming into the camp.

He found the country rich and fertile. "The land under the management of Northern farmers and free labor would be very productive." He estimated that 3/5ths to 4/5ths of the white population was inferior to the colored population in intelligence, with the exception of the very wealthy...."The whites are ignorant, bigoted and degraded. Slaves can't read or write because they are not taught. The whites can't because they are too indolent."

Capt. Milliman expected that they would be in Fredericksburg as soon as the pontoon bridges arrived. Food is expensive in the south, he wrote, except hoe cakes and fish. (Officers were paid for food, but had to supply their own mess.)

A system of (slave) impressments was in effect there. Five hundred (slaves) were drafted from the area, 300 deserted and hid out in the woods, but 200 were rounded up by secesh cavalry. "Upon our approach, the cavalry drove them across the bridge at us with swords."

Contrabands say their masters told them that the Union soldiers were coming to take them to Cuba and that they all had horns on their heads.

Capt. Milliman would die from wounds received at 2nd Bull Run (Manassas).

In April, General Hunter proclaimed all slaves within his command to be free.

Crocker responded to Pres. Lincoln's repudiation of General Hunter: "Lincoln's policy will be followed, offering the border states an easy way out of slavery, intimating that the time may not be too far distant when, if they refuse to embrace his offer, the necessities of the case will require him... to adopt a policy that will prove to them the thunderbolts of Jove; rather than the gentle dews of Heaven."

WHAT TO DO
WITH SLAVES

At the time of the Peninsula Campaign, serious thought was given to deportation of the freed slaves.

What to do with the millions of freed, former slaves was a question that troubled both the North and the South. Lincoln at one point favored shipping them to another country. Liberia, on the west coast of Africa, was founded with ex-slaves so exported. In June, 1862 the Danish charge d'affair suggested the Island of St. Croix, where U.S. former slaves could work beside native blacks at compensatory wages. The governor of the Danish West Indies sent an envoy to Washington to make the arrangements.

Sec'y of War Seward said that he was not authorized to enter into such an agreement, but that Congress in future might authorize it.

In July, 1862, after McClellan's miserable performance on the peninsula, Lincoln issued a call for 300,000 more "volunteers" to crush the Confederacy. These men would serve for three years or the duration of the war.

As the South had from the beginning, the Union now found great difficulty in securing soldiers. The first blush of patriotism that had propelled the "true believers" of Old Cambridge into the 22nd NY Vols, had suffered a seizure and died, victim at a stroke of the terribly sanguine war.

Never again would the North enjoy the luxury of a truly volunteer army. From July, 1862, most of the Union soldiers would be impressed from among European immigrants fresh off the boat and looking for work, and from among freed slaves.

Any old stock Anglo-Saxons who went would be wooed not by zeal or the dream of adventure, but by the mighty dollar: bounties, that routinely promised the equivalent of a years wages, just for mustering into Federal service.

IN NAME ONLY

Old Cambridge, throughout the war, would steadfastly resist conscription, ostensibly because it would have been a mark against its honor. But the real reason was that the sons from affluent families would have been compelled to go. The system that eventually won the war was "volunteerism" in name only.

NY Gov. Edward D. Morgan set the quotas and districted the State. Local committees were appointed and regimental camps established, where the 'volunteers" were to report. Old Cambridge, like all of the other communities, was compelled to go deeply into debt for the first time since the Revolution. It would be decades after the war before the last loan was repaid.

The money would be used to PAY the "volunteers"; bonus money for filling the regional quotas, for a district that did not provide its quota of volunteers had to fill by conscription.

REJECT PAYING
FOR MANUMISSION

That summer, President Lincoln submitted to Congress a plan whereby any state that voluntarily abolished slavery within its bounds would be compensated in U.S. Treasury bills.

This plan was rejected by the Black Republicans in ascendancy there. It would have been, however, a major step toward ending the conflict at this time, as those Southerners with slaves considered them property like livestock and might have settled for a Federal "buy-out", similar to one offered Washington County dairy farmers in the late 1980s.

Antietam was fought in mid-September by the armies, once again combined under the command of McClellan. It was one of the bloodiest in the history of pitched battles.

Editor Crocker saw it as "a great and decisive victory." Like Lincoln, he knew that the North desperately needed a victory. Lincoln had decided to publish his historic Emancipation Proclamation on the heels of a great victory for the North. He had withheld after Second Bull Run, but with the stand-off at Antietam, decided that was the best he was likely to get under his present coterie of incompetent generals and published the document.

This was no time to hold a county fair, so the directors postponed it for a year.

Crocker published Lincoln's proclamation in late September, adding "that the cause of the rebellion is slavery, no sane man can deny."

A HOUSE AFIRE

In early May, Crocker editorialized that the country was at a critical point in the war. The issue of slavery continued to trouble Washington County. "There is no point in asking the origin of the fire that is burning your house," he wrote. "We must expend all of our energies to put it out, first."

"We have those among us," he admitted, Who can see no other issue in this struggle. That slavery is to receive its death blow is conceded by all.

But as it became more and more difficult to raise soldiers in the county, Crocker deftly shifted away from the slavery issue.

Each time there is a new draft, the issue of Slavery causes trouble in the county ranks, and each time the liberal Crocker assures the Democrats that "even Jefferson Davis says that the war is for independence. "

Slavery, Crocker wrote, is an "incidental result" of the war.

"Every intelligent man knows that previous to this attempt to secede from the Union, the South enjoyed the full protection of the government in all of their constitutional rights, not excepting that of slavery.

"'Lincoln was in favor of saving the Union at all hazards, whether slavery went up or down."

Peace candidates were proclaiming it an ''abolitionist war." Crocker was well aware of the adverse effect of such statements upon the County recruiting.

"The assertion that this is an Abolition war" is a lie and a fraud," he trumpeted, "Invented by political demagogues and peace Democrats."

Andrew Johnston, who succeeded to the presidency upon Lincoln's death, announced a pardon to all participants in the Rebellion, restoring all rights and property, except their former slaves, provided they would take the oath of allegiance to the United States.

He was also down on "the political agitators, never content with FOLLOWING public sentiment, but ever seeking to create it or force it into some unnatural channel."

He was concerned over what to do with the slaves. The Black Republican radicals alarmed him. "They are determined to keep the irrepressible Negro in the advance, by demanding his right to immediate and universal suffrage to those who have been kept deliberately ignorant."

"Before he is enfranchised, a man should first be able to Read and have knowledge of the issues," he declared. But the Black Republicans didn't listen and Abraham Lincoln was no longer at the helm to steer them to a moderate course.

In December of 1865, prominent local Lawyer H.K. Sharpe concluded, "It is enough for one generation to have freed the slaves. The rest depends upon the negroes themselves."

Two years later, in November 1867, Editor Smart took Democrats to task for their motto, "A White Man's Government".

"That the affairs of the Republic have been administered in the interest of the Caucasian race during 80 yr. of its past is beyond civil.... That different views were held as to the propriety of holding the inferior race in bondage is true, but there is no evidence that they differed at all in the belief of the supremacy of the White Race."

Smart agreed with the Democrats. "This is a white man's government and the sentiment of the American people is to keep it such. It is the true policy of the Republic."

The fallacy of the Democrats is that they think Republicans disagree on this. The question in dispute is: Can the Negro vote without endangering this principle (a white man's government).

"If the African race can be made equal in all the rights of citizenship with the white without disturbing materially the preponderance of the Caucasian element in government, then undoubtedly this is the best policy to pursue.
"This is the belief of the Republican Party."
"If, on the other hand, such a course as claimed by Democrats weakens the power of the whites, then indeed have we made a mistake, fatal unless undone."

Smart was raised in Coila, the son of a Congregationalist minister. He served in the Civil War as a captain of artillery.

After the Civil War, he bought the Washington County Post from R.K. Crocker. The Post would be his springboard to a term in the U.S. Congress, the only local to be so elevated in politics.

In May 1868, Editor Smart saw the growth
of Klan power in the South a truer reading of
the political situation than votes (by blacks)
on the new Southern, state constitutions.

"Secret political societies are at all
times contra to the spirit of Republicanism,"
Smart thought. He applied this thinking to all
secret orders, including Freemasonry, with which
he frequently jousted in Cambridge.

Miscegenation

One aspect of freeing the slaves that was
particularly nettlesome involved sex between the
races. While it is pretty much acknowledged that
white masters often sired children with their
black female slaves, the idea that white women
could find black men attractive seemed to
astonish (and certainly to outrage) certain
white males.

In November, 1867, the first of two
reported incidents of miscegenation in Greenwich
were somewhat gleefully reported in the Old
Washington County Post:
" It seems that a Miss Lizzie Ames gave her
"blooming youth" to one Augustus Deridder, "an
ebony colored youth, in the bands of holy
matrimony."

The boys about Greenwich turned out in
force. They ravaged the ears of guests with
"melodics backed by symphonious pans and
melodious kettles."

Alderman Schuyler and Officer Spencer
talked the boys out of riding the groom out of
town on a rail. They rescued Deridder and
dispersed the boys.

In February, 1868, Heny Hogeboom, "the Negro who ran off with a Mrs. Hyde of Greenwich" encountered some difficulties. One evening "roughs" took him from the house where he was staying and rode him through main street Greenwich on a rail, dropping him in front of The Blakeley House (Inn), where he was generally assaulted by the mob.

Abe Lasher, Ephraim Burch and David Gleason were sentenced to 20 days in jail for the incident, but released when it was ascertained that the sentencing JP had no jurisdiction over the area.

In April 1878, George Welch, characterized as a "young loafer", obtained a room in a new carriage shop opened recently east of the Post (probably somewhere along Railroad south of the Jerome Wright building). He opened a billiard room and saloon in it.

Welch's mother visited to see how the boy was doing. She and another matron stepped in the door at midnight to find Welch and a number of other youths enjoying the society and caresses of "a couple of black wenches". The indignant mother closed the saloon for the night!

For some years, the Center Cambridge Hotel was the scene of Negro dances that drew a regional colored clientele. T.W. Hill was the proprietor after the Civil War. In December, 1868, "Quite a large party came on the (RR) cars and were carried over in Stroud's (the Union House proprietor) omnibus sleigh."

Eventually, the local residents would become so incensed with the carryings-on at the Center Cambridge Hotel that when it finally failed for lack of "custom", the Ingraham family, who lived where the Thomas family farmed in 2002, bought it, razed it and plowed the ground. In order to erase every vestige of it, they did everything biblical except to sow the ground with salt. It must have stood approximately where the town highway garage is today.

By May 1883, some place names in the area were changing. From the WCP: "What we know today as Lincoln Hill was then known as "Nigger Hill" and spoken of in the same disparaging breath with "Cobbtown" and "Pumpkin Hook," where there swelled poorly regarded white populations."

FREDERICK DOUGLAS

The famed half-breed Frederick Douglas drew mixed reviews in his appearances in Cambridge Village, especially after he married a white woman.

The winter of 1868, Editor Smart was in Frederick Douglas's corner when he spoke at the White Presbyterian Church. Editor Smart called Douglas "Not only one of the most forcible and sarcastic of living orators, but also one of the most polished and cultivated men in the country."

After his prepared lecture on the subject, "William the Silent," the Prince of Orange, Smart's assessment:

The White Church was filled. "Douglas was not as effective giving a prepared lecture as when speaking from the heart, but had a cold and a bronchial infection. This necessitated a very quiet delivery."

Miscegenation continued to be feared and opposed by the white population. When Frederick Douglas did this in 1884, the estimation of him by then Congressman Smart went down considerably:

"Frederick Douglas, the well-known leader of the colored people of the country, has married a white woman. The (Washington County) Post feels that coloreds will perceive this selfish action as distasteful, albeit constitutional. "It seems now that the race prejudice that is objectionable is the black man's prejudice against the whites, and not the whites against the blacks.

"It is perhaps hardly fair to expect the mass of the negroes to be logical, but surely the leaders among them might be expected to be so.

"In the ante-bellum days when all other arguments failed to deter a northern white man from becoming an abolitionist, he would ask, 'Do you want your daughter to marry a nigger?' A quarter century has not passed, but the situation seems reversed.

"The black man says to his fellows, 'Do you want your son to marry a white girl?'...The time may, and we are not sure but it ought to, come when color of complexion will cease to divide the human race, but the black man seems to be in no haste about it, as Douglas finds to his cost."

CONTRIBUTIONS OF

BLACK CITIZENS

It is unfortunately not within the limited powers of this writer to fairly chronicle the contributions to this community that have been made by its black citizens. But hopefully, the following material will be viewed by the reader as an effort in that direction. And hopefully, future researchers will exhibit due diligence in the furtherance of this effort.

Much of what follows is the result of a prolonged examination of the microfilm of the old, Washington County Post weekly newspaper. There may be more frustrating and time-consuming sources of historic data, but I haven't found them.

Suffice that it was, on my part, a labor of both love and respect.

dt

COLORED BASEBALL

In 1904, during the time when the Color Barrier kept the fine black athletes out of Major League Baseball, colored baseball teams barnstormed the country. One team called "The Cuban Giants" passed through this area each summer, playing the local boys.

George Hollister of Cambridge was at that time coaching the Granville town team. He was the best ball player to come out of Cambridge in the early days. Hollister brought his Granville nine down to the Cambridge fairgrounds to play the Cuban Giants, in hopes of a good pay-day for all.

The Giants let Hollister's charges win 6-3. This set up the bets for the match in Granville the following week. There The Cuban Giants trashed the Granville white boys 13-3.

Other colored teams, like the Windsor 9 of Troy enjoyed coming up to Cambridge and taking on the locals.

COLORED ENTERTAINMENT

Much local entertainment came by way of Negro performers. Many were touring acts that would play at Hubbard's Hall and The Cambridge Valley Fair. Churches would host choirs from black colleges.

At the 1904 Cambridge Fair, the featured entertainment before the grandstand was The Alabama Troubadours, 25 colored artists, singers, musicians and acrobats, said to be well worth the price of admission.

Or if one preferred, behind the grandstand one could watch Winston's Trained Seals and Sea lions.

In 1912, "Uncle Tom's Cabin" still toured on the vaudeville circuit, and still played in the Village at Hubbard's Hall. It had played the Hall annually since Civil War times. But to attract a 20th century crowd, the troupe had to resort to an afternoon parade on Main St., featuring the band, the ponies, the donkeys and the blood hounds.

And one must not neglect the impact of touring jazz musicians during the "Roaring 20s" and later, many of whom were black. In those days, the Jackson Ponds were sprinkled with "road houses" that provided live entertainment on weekends and holidays. Many elderly locals remember dancing to the music of these talented colored men.

LOCAL BURIALS

Buried in our local cemetery are several black men who served as soldiers in the Civil War in the Union cause.
Buried are former slaves who returned from that war with local white soldiers. Also buried in our local cemeteries are a host of black citizens who have been our servants, our co-workers, and, above all, our friends over the two hundred years of local history that this writer chronicles.

Many of their stories have yet to be told.

CIVIL WAR VETERANS

WARREN CHASE

Warren W. Chase was the best known of the colored Civil War veterans. Sgt. Chase served in Co. B, 20th Regt. Colored Infantry. He is buried under a marble, government issue stone in the northeast section of Woodlands.

Chase was for 20 years sexton of the Baptist Church, a position he resigned shortly before his death.

Chase was a member of the John McKie Post, Grand Army of the Republic. For many years, he carried the U.S. Flag at the head of the Post in the Memorial Day parade.

He liked to say that he had the honor of being the first colored soldier who had the authority to tell a white man what to do. When he was on duty at Jefferson City, La. in 1864, Gen. Ben Butler was tightening the screws on the rebellious civilian population.

Butler ordered all hotels and saloons closed at 9 p.m.

When Chase set out to enforce the new regulation, the first landlord he came to challenged him. Indignantly, the te man wanted to know by what authority a Negro could order a white hotel keeper to close.

Chase drew himself up in his blue uniform and replied, by the authority of Provost Capt. H.H. Rouse and the United States of America.

The proprietor closed his saloon.

In 1909, Warren Chase sought an increase in his Civil War pension, based upon his age. His pension was increased to $20 per month. In 1913, after 20 yrs. as sexton for the Baptist Church, Warren Chase resigned.

In March, 1915, Warren W. Chase died at his home on Maple Ave. He had been ill through the winter. He was 81, having been born in Salem. He lived most of his life in Cambridge Village.

LEWIS CHASE
C/W SOLDIER

Lewis P. Chase, apparently Warren's brother, was also a C/W soldier. He died of disease at Hart's Island Nov. 11, 1865 and is listed on the monument in the Soldiers Lot, Section I, Woodlands Cemetery.

LOCAL COMMANDED
COLORED TROOPS

Ebenezer Edgerton, a local resident, had the distinction of commanding colored troops in the Civil War. When the government finally relented and allowed blacks and former slaves to fight, it staffed the regiments with white officers. Edgerton, who died in the war, was a 1st Lt. in the 7th U.S. Colored Regt.

SMITH WINNIE
C/W SOLDIER

Smith Winnie Served in the 20th U.S. Colored Regt. He was born in White Creek March 1829 (estimate). He is buried in Woodlands Cemetery in Section B. Smith Winney died Oct. 29, 1899 of paralysis. He was born in White Creek in March 1829 (estimate). He is buried in Woodlands Cemetery in Section B, lot 309. Next of kin were Joseph Winney and Ellen "Bedon". The last name of Ellen could be a variation of "Bedeau", and suggests that there might be a connection between the ongoing, Winnie line and that of the old 1st Presbyterian Sexton and former slave, Salem Bedeau.

Mrs. Winnie was awarded in August, 1900 a pension of $8 per month, plus back pay.

WILLIAM JOHNSON
C/W SOLDIER

Wm. M. Johnson, colored Civil War veteran from Coila, died in October 1908. He was 81 and a life-long area resident. He served in the 20th US Colored Troops. He lies in Woodlands Cemetery, Section B, Lot 252.

The remains of Mrs. Williams (formerly Mrs. Johnson), colored, were brought to the Village for burial in January, 1902. Place of burial is unknown.

Mrs. Fannie Gifford (colored) died at her home on Academy St. on April 22, 1903, of consumption.

RETURN WITH FREEDMEN

There were several instances where local officers returned from the Civil War with black servants, who were then classified as Freedmen, who had been slaves under the Confederacy.

JESSE JONES

Capt. James Hill of Jackson, who served in the Washington County Regt. brought back from the Civil War one Jesse Jones.

Jones was supposed to have been born in Tennessee. He was a vigorous young man when first brought from the south. At the time, Capt. Hill said that Jones had been the slave of Confederate General Robert E. Lee.

His death was attributed to apoplexy. When Jesse Jones died September 6, 1898, he received a Presbyterian funeral, but his bones were placed to molder in an unmarked grave in the poor lot of Woodlands Cemetery.

WILLIAM WILLIS
HOOSICK SEXTON

Freed slaves were often as much at a loss as to what to do with themselves as were the Union soldiers who freed them. They joined the hundreds of sutlers and other "camp followers" in trekking behind their emancipators, often performing menial tasks about camp in exchange for simple considerations such as sustenance. In the case of William Willis, he made a brilliant choice by latching onto Col. Wm. B. Tibbits' brigade. Tibbits was from a wealthy Town of Hoosick family.

In November, 1894, William Willis, the colored sextant of All Saint's Episcopal Church, Hoosick, died of blood poisoning from a foot injury. He was born a slave in Culpepper Courthouse, Va. on the plantation of Robert Willis, from whom he took his name.

He latched onto the brigade of Col. Wm. B. Tibbits of Hoosick Falls at it fought in the Shenandoah Valley of Virginia in l864, and then followed Tibbits to service in the west, at Forts Kearney and Leavenworth.

In l865, Willis was sent to Hoosick with Tibbit's horses. There he became a part of the Tibbits household, was baptized in the All Saint's Church and spent the rest of his life as their sextant and general caterer to the congregation.

SALEM BEDEAU

Old Cambridge had its own slave sexton. Salem Bedeau was the sexton for the Old White Church that stood where Rite Aid is today. It is the same congregation, however, that occupies the great, white church that in 2002 stood opposite Rite Aid on the west side of North Park St. Salem was born a slave at Seabrook, Connecticut in about l767.

He came to be owned by Jeremiah Stillwell of Cambridge. All we know of Salem is the little that was recorded when he was manumitted by Stillwell on August 24, l810.

Salem was 5 ft. 8 inches in height. Once freed, Salem served as church sexton until his death in September, l858. His remains lie under a simple stone in the southeast corner of the Park St. burying ground, Village of Cambridge.

AS LOCAL SERVANTS

Negroes as servants have played major roles among the wealthy who have from time to time inhabited these hills. One example is the Adams family. They live and prosper in Cambridge to this day.

In February, 1908 Ulysses Grant Adams and family moved to Coila to work on the farm of Mrs. G.G. Wright. She was the daughter of 19th century capitalist George Law, and the farm Ulysses Grant Adams was to work on was, of course, Content Farm, a large complex of land and buildings north of the Village.

MISS JANET

BELOVED DOMESTIC

On December 29, 1901, died Miss Janet Santos of Coila. She was 97. Her father was Anthony Santos, "a Portugee". She was born in Coila and baptized by Dr. Alexander Bullions, the first principal of the Cambridge Washington Academy. With six brothers and sisters, she lived in the house that was occupied in January 1902, by William Johnson, a colored man. Her family all moved west "in the early days of immigration."

For years, Miss Janet was the domestic in the house of John Robinson. For the last 29 years of her life she served in the house of William Shiland. She also worked 16 years in the house of John Green. She so endeared herself as a servant that the families cared for her until her death.

Mrs. Warren Vincent, colored, died April 16, 1907, of consumption (tuberculosis; a common killer in those days). She had been born in Vermont in 1861. She was buried in Woodlands in section A, lots 209-211. Her relatives were Horace Putnam, Ursula James and Warren Vincent.

JOHN NEWCOMB

. In March, 1881, John Newcomb of White Creek was called to serve on the Washington County Grand Jury. He is believed to be the first grand jurist of color to be called in the history of the County.

PUBLIC BAPTISM

In July, 1883, a public baptism of a colored person was performed in the Seed House Brook behind the old Washington County Post building. Rev. Goodall of the Baptist Church performed the baptism. The woman was not named.

LAST COUNTY RESIDENT
BORN A SLAVE

Aunt Phila Weston, believed to be the last survivor of negroes born slaves in Washington County, died in November, 1891 at the county poorhouse. She was thought to be 100 yrs. old. She had removed to the poorhouse when she became ill. The poorhouse was where the old folks infirmary is south of Argyle today.

B. TRUE ROBINSON

In 1886, the custodian at the Academy School was B. Truman Robinson (Be True Robinson), a colored man with a good personality but a drinking problem. He was also employed part-time at the Old WCP. Following a "Printer's Ball", the Post reported Be True done in by the ball and the "weather". When the Union School opened, Be True was apparently one of the first janitors.

In March, 1894, he died of pneumonia. He had been sent to Bennington for treatment of his alcoholism a few days previous.He had been dried out for some time previous, apparently enjoying his job of school janitor.

He was well-liked, as much for his "often misdirected generosity" as for any other characteristic. "But we could not help him as we wanted to, so let it be a warning to men of the danger of an association with tipplers and tippling."

Be True left a young wife and several small children. All she had was $800 insurance on their Main St. house that had recently burned. However she was able to move into a new home on Gilmore Ave., where she lived out her days.

MORRIS DRIGGRISS SR.
CARRIED US FLAG

Although not a servant, at the turn of the century, Morris Drigus (Driggriss) Sr. always carried the U.S. Flag at the head of the grand floral procession on the last day of the Great Cambridge Fair. It was a tradition begun by colored Civil War soldier Warren Chase

When Driggriss carried the American Flag in the precession, the Fair's founder and President, Jerome B. Rice, would follow with some major out-of-town dignitary, often a Civil War general or the Governor of New York or Vermont. While Morris Driggriss proudly marched, Rice--- the crippled Civil War Veteran--- and the dignitary would be conveyed in the latest technological breakthrough in personal transportation.

BILLY WICKS

One of the more famous Negro servants in local history was Billy Wicks.
He was the life-long servant of Jerome Bonaparte Rice. He began his service with Jerome's father, Nathan. Then after five years he began his life work of caring for the crippled Industrialist.

Jerome Rice took over the family seed business and built it into the second largest seed company in the United States, with trial gardens and processing plants throughout the United States.

He was also the man behind The Great Cambridge Fair. He headed
the group of businessmen who built the Cambridge Waterworks, and he provided the land upon which was built The Union School.

The young Jerome Rice was an enlisted man in the 123rd New York Volunteers, the so-called "Washington County Regt.", He was captured at the battle of Chancellors Ville. While captive in Libby Prison, Richmond, Virginia, he was subjected to cold and extremely damp conditions. This is thought to be what brought on his crippling arthritis.

During the post productive period of his life J.B. Rice was confined to a "go cart" or what we have come to call a wheeled chair.

It was the black man, Billy Wicks, who was always behind the wheeled chair of Jerome Rice.

Billy Wicks died August 26, 1937, at the age of 81. His wife and
their only child, a daughter, had died years before.

J.B. Rice was so grateful for the faithful service of this man that he had built for the Wicks family a home on the seed house grounds.

Billy Wicks was buried from Jerome Rice's church, the Methodist Episcopal seen today on Main St. His body was placed in Woodlands Cemetery.

A few years ago a woman visited Cambridge seeking information on the "Weeks", a line of her family tree. As town historian I was pointed out as a possible source of information.

The woman was from Massachusetts. She drove an expensive automobile. She held a PhD degree and was an educator. She was also black.

I was of little help, initially, in that I knew of no black Weeks family in Cambridge history. But as he was still living then and widely recognized as a fount of both local history and wisdom, I sent her in search of one of the most beloved colored men of our generation, Morris Driggriss Jr. of Coila and Jackson. It didn't take Morris long to solve the mystery.

"Weeks," he pronounced. "Weeks". Then he let it slide. "Wicks, WICKS"! And the good lady had found her distant, Cambridge connection.

PHOEBE WICKS

In November of 1916, Miss Phoebe Elizabeth Wicks, S. Pearl St. resident, died at age 39. She was a violinist "of note". She may have been a daughter of Billy Wicks, and the S. Pearl St. house in which she died likely was the one Jerome B. Rice built for and gave to his beloved manservant, Billy.

#

www.ingramcontent.com/pod-product-compliance
Lightning Source LLC
Chambersburg PA
CBHW072038060426
42449CB00010BA/2332